The
Marriage
Preparation
Course

Guest Manual

Published by Alpha International, HTB Brompton Road, London SW7 1JA.

publications@alpha.org

Contents

This manual is designed to be used on
The Marriage Preparation Course with
the DVDs or live talks. See page 51 for
more information on how to join or run
a course.

Communication

The value of marriage preparation

Knowing how to make a marriage work
- Marriage is the most exciting and the most challenging adventure we can undertake
- Strong marriages don't develop automatically
- Over 40 per cent of marriages in the UK break down
- Best way to insure a marriage is to invest in it

Learning the necessary skills
- How to communicate effectively
- How to resolve conflict
- How to meet each other's emotional needs
- How to build a friendship
- How to develop our sexual relationship
- How to determine roles

Becoming aware of the differences between us
- Different expectations
- Our upbringing
- Cultural differences
- Learning to communicate
- Communication involves talking and listening effectively
- Process of learning how to be good communicators

Learning to communicate

Communication involves talking and listening effectively
- Process of learning how to be good communicators

Our communication is affected by:

1. Our personality
- Extrovert or introvert
- Logical or intuitive

EXERCISE 1

How We Communicate

Tell your fiancé(e) how you think their personality impacts the way they communicate.

---

2. Our family background
- Some families air differences immediately/others delay
- Some are quiet/others are much louder
- Some are more volatile/others are calmer
- Some take it in turns to talk/others frequently interrupt

3. Our circumstances
- Job
- Children
- Pressures from outside and within our marriage

Barriers to effective communication

1. Insufficient time
- Set aside time for meaningful conversation on a regular basis
- Plan this time (it doesn't just happen)
- Planned time prevents a backlog of non-communication or mis-communication
- Recognise when to drop everything and listen

EXERCISE 2

Family Styles of Communication

Complete the following exercise on your own and then talk about it together. Mark with an 'x' where you think your own family comes on the line between the two extremes

Overall the communication in my family was:

Indirect ———————————————————————— Direct

Indirect   Direct

Vague   Specific

Relaxed   Stressful

Non-confrontational   Confrontational

Closed   Open

Loud   Quiet

Humorous   Serious

How has the way your family communicated when you were growing up affected the way you communicate now as an adult? How different is this to the way your fiancé(e)'s family communicates?

2. Failing to talk about our feelings

- Danger of communicating only about practical things or at the most superficial level
- Sharing our innermost thoughts and feelings is essential for a strong marriage
- Some people find talking about their feelings difficult because of inadequacy, vulnerability or fear
- Dare to trust your fiancé(e) and start disclosing your feelings to him or her
- Listen to each other without judging or criticising

EXERCISE 3

Effective Talking

Ask your fiancé(e) how difficult or easy it is for them to talk about their inner thoughts, attitudes and emotions. Find out if they were encouraged to talk about their feelings during their upbringing.

---

3. Holding on to hurt and resentment

- Tell each other when and why you are feeling resentful
- Listen and try to understand
- Keep apologising and forgiving

Notes

4. Failing to listen to each other

- Listening is costly
- Listening demands time and patience
- Recognise and overcome bad habits such as:
  - interrupting
  - going off at a tangent
  - giving advice
- Effective listening is something we can all learn and practise
- Put aside your own agenda and try to see the world through your fiancé(e)'s eyes
- Make the effort to understand your fiancé(e) when they think or feel differently

'This means not just listening with your ears, but also more importantly, listening with your eyes and your heart, listening for feeling, for meaning.'
Stephen Covey
The Seven Habits of Highly Effective People

EXERCISE 4

Effective Listening

1. Ask your fiancé(e) to tell you about something that is worrying them. Listen carefully.

2. Reflect back what they have said, particularly about their feelings, to show that you have understood. If you did not understand, your fiancé(e) should tell you again.

3. Then ask, 'What's concerning you most about what you've told me?'

4. Again, reflect back what they say.

5. Then ask, 'Is there anything you could do (or, if appropriate, you'd like me or us to do) about what you've just said?'

6. Again, reflect back what they say.

7. Finally ask, 'Is there anything else you would like to say?' Then swap roles.

'The gift of being a good listener, a gift which requires constant practice is perhaps the most healing gift anyone could possess. It doesn't judge or advise the other, but communicates support at a level deeper than words.'
Gerard Hughes

Session 1 – Homework

EXERCISE

Write down your answers to the following questions and then discuss them with your fiancé(e).

1. Are you a good listener?
   On a rating of 1 to 10 score your ability as a listener:
   1☐ 2☐ 3☐ 4☐ 5☐ 6☐ 7☐ 8☐ 9☐ 10☐

2. How would you rate your fiancé(e)?
   1☐ 2☐ 3☐ 4☐ 5☐ 6☐ 7☐ 8☐ 9☐ 10☐

3. When have you had the best conversations about your deepest thoughts and emotions? Which times and places are most conducive to good communication?

   _____

   _____

4. What have been the worst times and places for communicating effectively? Can you work out why?

   _____

   _____

5. Complete the following: I find it easier to be open and vulnerable with you when you...

   _____

2 ▶ Commitment

Why marriage?

- Trends in our culture causing marriage breakdown:
  - consumerism
  - 'throw-away' mentality
- Current research shows benefits of stable marriages to individuals and society
- The biblical view:
  'For this reason a man will leave his father and mother and be united to his wife and the two will become one flesh'
  (Genesis 2:24)
- Marriage – a vital part of God's design for human society

Alvin Toffler, the sociologist and best-selling author, wrote that people today have a 'throw-away' mentality. They not only have throw-away products but they make throw-away friends and it is this mentality which produces throw-away marriages.

Two purposes of marriage:

1. Friendship
- *'It is not good for the man to be alone'*
  (Genesis 2:18)
- Marriage isn't the only way to counter aloneness but is the closest human relationship
- Marriage meets our longing for intimacy

2. Family life

- Ideal is for children to grow up seeing an intimate, committed, long-term relationship between their parents
- Breakdown of marriage has effect on next generation
- A strong marriage can break the cycle of failed relationships

---

EXERCISE 1

The Benefits of Marriage

Discuss between the two of you: What, in your view, is the role of marriage in society? Why are you choosing marriage rather than cohabitation?

The marriage covenant

- Infatuation versus lasting love
- Difference between a contract and a covenant
- Commitment is protective casing around our relationship
- Intimacy requires vulnerability
- Vulnerability requires trust
- Trust requires commitment
- Your wedding vows express commitment to each other

'Love and faithfulness meet together.'

Psalm 85:10

EXERCISE 2

The Marriage Vows

Read through the Marriage Service vows together and decide which is the most important phrase for each of you. Explain your choice to your fiancé(e) (see Appendix 3).

Spending time together

- Make it happen – through planning
- Organise change of routine and do something special
- Creates opportunities for effective communication
- Keeps romance, love and fun alive

Suggested ways to make time together:

1. Daily basis

- Connect with each other every day
- Choose best time of day
- Create habits

2. Weekly basis

- 'Date night' or 'marriage time' once a week
- Plan marriage time (write it in your diaries)
- Make marriage time a priority over other demands
- Protect marriage time from interruptions (friends/family/ telephone)

3. Annual basis

- Mini-honeymoon each year
- Plan holidays
- These help revitalise our relationship and rekindle romance

Notes

EXERCISE 3

Planning Time Together

Discuss when you will spend time together investing in your marriage on a daily/weekly/annual basis.

Write down your plans:

- _____

- _____

- _____

- _____

The change of loyalties

Notes

1. Leaving
- The new centre of gravity – physical, psychological and emotional leaving
- Church wedding service may include symbolic leaving
- New decision-making structure
- Marriage relationship takes priority
- Make your own decisions and support each other

2. Respecting our parents
- Showing gratitude
- Staying in touch
- Taking the initiative
- Deciding together on level of contact
- Planning for major festivals

3. Arranging the wedding

- Hard work!
- An emotional process
- Be prepared to compromise

'When a husband and wife have an agreed policy and stand firmly together putting it into effect, attempts at exploitation and manipulation invariably fail: But any weakness, any crack in the unity of husband and wife enables the in-laws to drive a wedge in between.'

David Mace

EXERCISE 4

Parents and In-laws

Discuss as a couple:

From the following list, what possible areas of tension can you foresee with your parents/parents-in-law?

1. Holidays	5. Frequency of visits
2. Christmas/other festivals	6. Length of telephone calls
3. Finances	7. Changed loyalty
4. Interference	8. Other...

How could they be resolved?

Allowing time apart

Two dangers:

1. Too much time apart
- Not enough shared interests

2. No space to pursue separate interests
- Some time apart is healthy for a marriage
- Requires mutual agreement and consent
- Brings fresh interests and stories into a marriage
- Renews our desire to be back together
- Need to find balance between time together and time apart

Notes

Session 2 – Homework

EXERCISE
Time Apart

Each write down any individual interests you expect to pursue without your fiancé(e):

1. _____

2. _____

3. _____

How frequently and how much time would these take?

1. _____

2. _____

3. _____

Write down any individual interests you expect your fiancé(e) to pursue without you:

1. _____

2. _____

3. _____

Please turn over →

EXERCISE (continued)

How frequently and how much time might these take?

1. _____

2. _____

3. _____

Now compare and discuss your answers.

3 Resolving Conflict

Expecting conflict

- We're different
- We're all naturally selfish
- We've moved from independence to interdependence

Handling anger

- Anger is not wrong in itself
- Two ways we can use anger inappropriately
  - rhinos: explode
  - hedgehogs: bury anger
- Both are damaging and ineffective ways of resolving conflict

EXERCISE
Rhinos and Hedgehogs
Ask yourself if you have rhino or hedgehog tendencies when you are angry. If you are not sure, check with your fiancé(e) who may have a better idea!

Recognising Your Differences

1. Mark against each issue where on the line your partner's and your own preferences each lie, *eg (N = Nicky; S = Sila).*

Money
$$\overset{\displaystyle S \qquad\qquad\qquad\qquad\qquad N}{\rule{18cm}{0.4pt}}$$
Spend   Save

ISSUE	PREFERENCE	
Money	Spend	Save
Holidays	Adventure	Rest
People	Spend time with others	Spend time alone
Sleeping	Go to bed late	Get up early
Tidiness	Keep everything tidy/under control	Be relaxed/live in a mess
Disagreements	Thrash it out	Keep the peace
TV	Keep it on	Throw it out
Relaxation	Go out	Be at home
Punctuality	Have time in hand	Cut it fine
Planning	Make plans/stick to them	Be flexible/change plans
Organisation	Organised	Disorganised
Decisions	Spontaneous	Cautious
Family	See often	See rarely
Friends	Long list	A few close ones
Music	Like it on contantly	Only at certain times

EXERCISE 1 (continued)

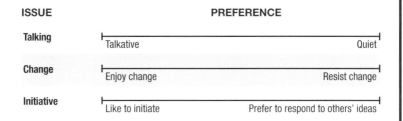

ISSUE	PREFERENCE	
Talking	Talkative	Quiet
Change	Enjoy change	Resist change
Initiative	Like to initiate	Prefer to respond to others' ideas

Do it separately and then compare answers.

2. Discuss how your differences can be complementary in your relationship.

Accepting our differences

- Recognise and accept your differences
- Differences can be complementary
- One attitude is not better or worse – just different
- Can't expect to change each other
- Appreciate each other's strengths
- Support each other's weaknesses

Notes

Looking for solutions

Look for a solution together rather than attack, surrender or bargain.

Six steps for resolving conflict effectively

1. Hit the 'pause' button
- Is this a good time? (the 'ten o'clock rule')
- Is this a good place?

2. Identify the issue
- Take the issue that is causing conflict from between you
- Put it out in front of you
- Move towards each other to work on it together

3. Discuss the issue rather than attack each other
- Learn to control temper
- Avoid labelling, eg: 'you always...'/ 'you never...'
- Use 'I' statements, eg: 'I feel hurt when...'

4. Listen to each other
- Try to understand each other's perspective
- Take it in turns to talk

5. Work out possible solutions
- Talk about different possibilities
- May help to write a list

6. Choose the best solution for your relationship and see if it works
- If it doesn't, try another solution
- If you can't find a solution together, ask for help

Using the Six Steps

1. What patterns of resolving (or failing to resolve) conflict did you observe in your parents' marriage?

2. What are the trigger points for conflict in your relationship?

3. What causes conflict to escalate and what helps each of you to hit the 'pause' button?

4. Which is the most important of the 'Six steps for resolving conflict' for each of you?

Dealing with finances

- Marriage involves sharing everything
- Set aside time to discuss finances
- Different attitudes to finances can cause tension
- Decide who will manage the finances
- Recognise your different attitudes to money (are you more of a 'saver' or a 'spender'?)
- Discover your true financial position
- Calculate your joint income
- Calculate/forecast your expenses
- Do a budget (discuss the balance of spending/saving/giving away)
- Guard against over-spending (watch the credit card)
- Discuss the repayment of any debts you have
- Talk openly about your feelings
- Developing a dynamic partnership requires:
  - honesty about the present
  - forgiveness for the past
  - agreement about the future

[See also: The Marriage Book, Appendix 3 'Working out a budget']

Notes

EXERCISE 3

Discussing Your Finances

Each of you fill in your answers to the following questions and then discuss what you have put.

1. Describe your attitude to shopping (tick appropriate boxes):

    ☐ source of pleasure

    ☐ like buying presents

    ☐ enjoy window shopping

    ☐ occasionally use it as escapism

    ☐ impulsive and sometimes wasteful

    ☐ only buy essentials

    ☐ depends on what I am buying,

    ☐ avoid whenever possible where and when

2. Do you worry about running out of money?   ☐ yes   ☐ no

3. Will you have a joint bank account?   ☐ yes   ☐ no

4. Will you keep separate accounts?   ☐ yes   ☐ no

5. How will you balance spending, saving and giving away?

6. Will you work out a budget?   ☐ yes   ☐ no

7. Can you keep control with a credit card?   ☐ yes   ☐ no

8. Are you in debt?   ☐ yes   ☐ no
    If so, by how much? _____

    Discuss your plans for repayment.

9. How much could each of you spend without consulting the other?

10. Who will manage your finances?

    ☐ jointly   ☐ husband   ☐ wife

Forgiving each other

Hurt is inevitable. There is a simple but powerful process for healing:

1. Identifying the hurt
- Tell your husband or wife when they have upset you

2. Learning to say sorry
- Pride can make it hard to say sorry
- Opens way for discussion and change

3. Forgiveness
- Forgiveness is one of the greatest forces for healing in a marriage

- Forgiveness IS NOT:
  - forgetting the hurt happened
  - pretending it doesn't matter
  - failing to confront our husband or wife's wrong and hurtful behaviour

- Forgiveness IS:
  - facing the wrong done to us
  - recognising the emotions inside
  - choosing not to hold the offence against our husband or wife
  - giving up our self-pity

- Forgiveness is first and foremost a choice, not a feeling
  - new feelings follow forgiveness
  - forgiveness deals with anger and resentment – although we might still feel hurt until healing is complete
  - forgiveness is a process – we often need to keep forgiving (sometimes on a daily basis)
  - we are to forgive out of gratitude for the forgiveness we have received

'Love keeps no record of wrongs.'

1 Corinthians 13:5

'The word resentment expresses what happens if the cycle of blame goes uninterrupted. It means literally, "to feel again": resentment clings to the past, relives it over nd over, picks each fresh scab so that the wound never heals.'

Philip Yancey,
What's So Amazing About Grace?

'Bear with each other and forgive whatever grievances you may have against one another. Forgive as the Lord forgave you.'

Colossians 3:13

Notes

Session 3 – Homework

EXERCISE

Agree on a suitable time and place to discuss one important issue that is causing disagreement between you.

1. Identify the issue

   _____

   _____

2. How have each of you responded to this issue in the past?

   Me _____

   You _____

3. Both write down what you consider the main concern you each have regarding the issue.

   Me _____

   You _____

   Discuss what you have each written down. Take it in turns to talk and be sure to listen to each other's point of view without blaming or criticising.

Please turn over →

EXERCISE (continued)

4. Brainstorm possible solutions – do not rule out any at this stage

1. _____

2. _____

3. _____

4. _____

5. Discuss the solutions to see which one would work best.

6. Try that solution. If it doesn't seem to work, go back to your list and try another one.

4 ▶ Keeping Love Alive

Developing our friendship

1. Friends confide in each other
- No secrets

2. Friends talk to each other
- Importance of meal times

3. Friends have fun together
- Shared experiences lead to shared memories and stimulate conversation

---

EXERCISE 1
Building Friendship

Write out a list of the activities you enjoy doing together now. How could you make sure you are still doing these things together five/ten/fifteen years into your marriage?

- _____
- _____
- _____
- _____
- _____

Discovering each other's needs

- Learn to recognise how each of you feels loved
- Five ways through which we can show and be shown love:

1. **Loving words**
2. **Quality time**
3. **Thoughtful presents**
4. **Physical affection**
5. **Kind actions**

(Taken from Gary Chapman's excellent book,
The Five Love Languages)

- Like different languages to communicate love
- One will communicate love to us more effectively than the others
- Often different for our fiancé(e)
- Common to try to communicate love in the way we understand it and want to receive it
- Need to learn our fiancé(e)'s love language(s)
- Takes effort, discipline and practice

Notes

Discover Your 'Love Languages'

Write down six specific occasions on which you have particularly known your fiancé(e)'s love for you.

I have known your love for me when:

1. _____

2. _____

3. _____

4. _____

5. _____

6. _____

Taking into consideration the six examples above, try to put the five ways of showing love in order of importance for you. Then consider which order you would put them in for your fiancé(e). When you have both finished, show each other what you have put.

For you Number 1–5 (1 = most important)	Love expressed through:	For your fiancé(e) Number 1–5 (1 = most important)
☐	Words	☐
☐	Time	☐
☐	Presents	☐
☐	Touch	☐
☐	Actions	☐

Building our sexual relationship

Sex

- Communication at the deepest levels of our personality
- A vital and integral part of marriage
- Given for our enjoyment not just procreation
- Good sex is other-focussed
- Destructive outside a committed relationship
- An expression of love within the commitment of marriage
- Involves the giving of ourselves to each other

'Do not awaken love until it so desires.'

Song of Songs
2:7; 3:5; 8:4

'Trust is one of the prime requirements for a good sex life. When a couple trusts one another they can enjoy giving and receiving, but when one person might use the other, there is a tension.'

Alan Storkey,
Marriage and its Modern Crisis

EXERCISE 3

Sex and Commitment

Discuss and agree on your own boundaries prior to marriage.

How to build your sexual relationship

Six secrets for keeping sex alive:

1. See it as a journey
- A discovery over a lifetime
- Importance of laughter
- Growing in understanding of each other
- Talk about expectations and any fears
- Plan a relaxing honeymoon
- Don't compartmentalise sex
- Sexual intimacy affects every other part of our marriage
- Sex is not just the icing on the cake – it's a vital ingredient of the cake itself

2. Be ready to talk
- Differences between male and female sexuality
- Sexual responses likely to be different
- Can be difficult to talk because deeply private and requires vulnerability
- Tell each other what turns you on and what turns you off
- Don't leave to guess work

3. Be prepared to tackle problems
- Most couples experience problems in their sexual relationship at some time
- Problems resulting from abuse or other sexual trauma from the past may require professional help (ask your course leader for advice)
- Other problems can usually be worked through together such as:
  - low self-esteem and poor body image
  - tiredness
  - different levels of desire
- Most problems couples experience are common
  - don't bury the problem
  - talk together
  - read a book on sex together to help you talk
  - problems do not equal failure
  - seek help if necessary

4. Deal with past sexual relationships

- Past relationships can cause jealousy and mistrust
- Recognise if this is an issue for either of you
- Be honest with each other
- Resolved through talking/forgiveness/ prayer
- Bring closure to past relationships
- May need to destroy letters/diaries/photos

5. Discuss family planning and having children

- Discuss both before you get married
- Come to a joint decision
- Children change the shape of a marriage relationship
- Read a book about family planning (see Appendix 5)

6. Don't believe everything you hear

- Avoid comparisons
- Every marriage is unique
- Physical relationship will change over the course of the marriage

Notes

EXERCISE 4

Talking About Sex

Talk together about whatever you think is important for you from this session to build a good sexual relationship.

Session 4 – Homework

EXERCISE
Making Decisions

This exercise will help you to prepare for Session 5.

In the left-hand column, write down who decided what in your parents' (or step-parents') marriage as a percentage of their influence (*eg: 50:50 or 70:30 or 90:10*). Then in the right-hand column put your expectations for your own marriage.

Discuss what you have each put. If you grew up with one parent, only fill in the right-hand column.

My parents		Decision to make	Our marriage	
Father	Mother		Husband	Wife
:		Choice of new car	:	
:		Choice of where to live	:	
:		Choice of furniture	:	
:		Choice of crockery	:	
:		Choice of own clothes	:	
:		Choice of holiday	:	

Please turn over

My parents		Decision to make	Our marriage	
Father	Mother		Husband	Wife
:		Choice of decoration of home	:	
:		Choice of pictures	:	
:		Choice of how to bring up children	:	
:		Choice of TV programmes	:	
:		Choice of food	:	
:		Choice of number of children	:	
:		Choice of husband's job	:	
:		Choice of wife's job	:	
:		Determining how money is spent	:	

5 Shared Goals and Values

Matching our strides

Marriage provides us with greatest opportunity and greatest challenge.
It involves:

1. Changing our behaviour
- Expecting to give more than we take
- Making sacrifices

2. Being healed of our past
- We may overreact as a result of our upbringing
- Need to look at our reactions and ask,
  'Is that reasonable?'
- Change is possible
  - involves talking about our own reactions
  - involves forgiving those who have hurt us or let us down in the past

Notes

3. Letting go of unrealistic expectations

- Marriage cannot meet all of our needs
- Unrealistic expectations lead to a downward spiral

4. Showing appreciation on a daily basis

- No marriage can survive lack of appreciation
- Expressing appreciation of each other even when we don't feel like it

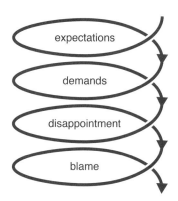

expectations

demands

disappointment

blame

EXERCISE 1

Expressing Appreciation

Write a list of your fiancé(e)'s strengths and the qualities you most admire in him or her:

1. _____

2. _____

3. _____

4. _____

5. _____

6. _____

7. _____

8. _____

Then take it in turns to read out to your fiancé(e) what you have each put.

Working out our values

- Our values determine our decisions and choices
- May have different personalities but same core values
- Talking about our dreams, aspirations, hopes and longings
- Putting our priorities in order

Consider the value you will put on:

1. Friendships
- Enrich our lives and marriage
- All our relationships need to be redefined

2. Children
- Can draw a couple closer together or push them apart
- Need to keep planning time together as a couple

3. Jobs
- Not competing with each other
- Encouraging each other
- Talking about what happens if and when we have children
- Good to talk about what we hope to achieve together –
  to develop a vision for our marriage

Notes

EXERCISE 2

Living Out Your Values

Each of you choose your five top values and put them in order.

Then put against each one how you hope to live out that value in the future. Use the list of examples below to help you but do not be limited by it. When you have finished, compare and discuss what you have each put.

Examples of values: health, creativity, marriage relationship, sport, vocation/ job, good stewardship of money and possessions, local community involvement, adventure, having fun, hospitality, friendships, care of environment, nurturing children, ongoing education, spirituality/relationship with God, wider family, generosity, church activities.

Examples of how you might plan to live out a value:
* *Relationship with God: seek to pray together for each other each day*
* *Our marriage relationship: set aside time each week to have fun together*

Value

1. _____ : _____

2. _____ : _____

3. _____ : _____

4. _____ : _____

5. _____ : _____

Creating an equal partnership

- We need to determine:
  - who does what
  - who decides what
  - who takes the lead in each area of our marriage
- Assumptions from our parents' marriage
- Talking about our expectations
- New Testament model
  - requires mutual giving to each other (see Appendix 2)
  - undermined male dominance
- The differences between male and female
  - which are the result of creation and which of culture?
  - male strength given to protect, not to dominate and oppress
- Designed to complement each other
  - submitting to one another is key to a loving marriage

'Submit to one another out of reverence for Christ.'

Ephesians 5:21

Working out roles within marriage
- Who is best suited to what?
- Roles will probably change over the years
- Roles and responsibility

EXERCISE 3
Roles and Responsibilities

1. Each write down up to to six areas for which you expect to take responsibility.
   For example: housework, cleaning the bathroom, taking out rubbish, cooking, paying bills, organising holidays, ironing, thank you letters, driving, map-reading, DIY, earning money, gardening, insurance, shopping...

   1. _____   4. _____

   2. _____   5. _____

   3. _____   6. _____

2. Each write down up to six areas for which you expect your fiancé(e) to take responsibility:

   1. _____   4. _____

   2. _____   5. _____

   3. _____   6. _____

3. Each write down up to six areas that you expect will be a joint responsibility:

   1. _____   4. _____

   2. _____   5. _____

   3. _____   6. _____

4. When you have finished, compare lists.

5. In which of these areas do you expect your fiancé(e) to take the lead in your marriage?

Building spiritual togetherness

As we receive from God we are able to give to each other.

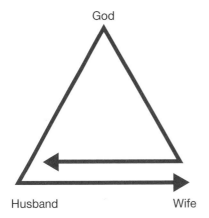

God

Husband   Wife

'A cord of three strands is not quickly broken.'

Ecclesiastes 4:12

Praying together for each other can bring great intimacy.

- Daily prayer – 'what can I pray for you today?'
- Focus on each other's needs
- Accept the same requests day after day
- Start with thankfulness
- Praying doesn't just happen – needs to be planned

EXERCISE 4

Spiritual Togetherness

Tell each other what the diagram of the triangle above means to you, if anything, and whether you'd like to pray together regularly.

Session 4 – Homework

EXERCISE
Putting it into Practice

Three things I especially want to remember and practise from The Marriage Preparation Course:

1. _____

2. _____

3. _____

Show your fiancé(e) what you have written.

Now ask him/her, 'What three things would you especially like me to remember and practise from the course?' Write them down here:

1. _____

2. _____

3. _____

Appendix 1

Ready for marriage?

(see *The Marriage Book* – Appendix 1)

- **The sharing test**
  Do I want to share the rest of my life with my fiancé(e)?

- **The character test**
  Do I regard my fiancé(e) as being kind?

- **The strength test**
  Does our love give me energy and strength, or does it drain me?

- **The respect test**
  Do I respect my fiancé(e)?

- **The habit test**
  Do I accept my fiancé(e) as they are now (bad habits and all)?

- **The quarrel test**
  Are we able to admit our mistakes, apologise and forgive each other?

- **The interest test**
  Do we have interests in common as a foundation for friendship?

- **The time test**
  Have we weathered all the seasons and a variety of situations together?

These tests have been adapted from *I Married You* by Walter Trobisch (IVP, 1973).

If you are unable to answer yes to the questions above, we suggest you discuss your feelings with someone other than your fiancé(e).

Appendix 2

Ephesians 5:21–33

'21Submit to one another out of reverence for Christ. 22Wives, submit to your husbands as to the Lord. 23For the husband is the head of the wife as Christ is the head of the church, his body, of which he is the Saviour. 24Now as the church submits to Christ, so also wives should submit to their husbands in everything. 25Husbands, love your wives, just as Christ loved the church and gave himself up for her 26to make her holy, cleansing her by the washing with water through the word, 27and to present her to himself as a radiant church, without stain or wrinkle or any other blemish, but holy and blameless. 28In this same way, husbands ought to love their wives as their own bodies. He who loves his wife loves himself. 29After all, people have never hated their own bodies, but feed and care for them, just as Christ does the church – 30for we are members of his body. 31"For this reason a man will leave his father and mother and be united to his wife, and the two will become one flesh." 32This is a profound mystery – but I am talking about Christ and the church. 33However, each one of you must love his wife as he loves himself, and the wife must respect her husband.'

1. The context of the whole passage is: 'Submit to one another out of reverence for Christ' (Ephesians 5:21). (Submitting is the opposite of lording it over or seeking to control. Marriage is designed to be a relationship of mutual giving as we seek to serve each other and to put each other's needs ahead of our own.)

2. Compare the duties of husband and wife (more is written to the husband owing to the prevailing culture in which a husband had total rights over his household):
   - the husband's duty: *'Husbands, love your wives just as Christ loved the church and gave himself up for her... husbands ought to love their wives as their own bodies.'* (Ephesians 5:25,28).
   - the wife's duty: *'Wives, submit to your husbands as to the Lord'* (Ephesians 5:22).

3. 'Head' does not necessarily mean leader. St Paul could be emphasising the close connection between husband and wife in marriage. They cannot act independently of each other any longer.

4. Servant-leadership means taking responsibility rather than leaving the issue to our husband or wife: we should take the initiative rather than taking control.

5. The whole passage is set in the context of seeking God's will rather than seeking to impose our own will: *'Find out what pleases the Lord... understand what the Lord's will is'* (Ephesians 5:10,17).

Appendix 3

The marriage vows

The priest/minister says to the bridegroom:
[Name], will you take [Name] to be your wife? Will you love her, comfort her, honour and protect her, and, forsaking all others, be faithful to her as long as you both shall live?

He answers:
I will.

The priest/minister says to the bride:
[Name], will you take [Name] to be your husband? Will you love him, comfort him, honour and protect him, and, forsaking all others, be faithful to him as long as you both shall live?

She answers:
I will.

The priest/minister may receive the bride from the hand of her father. The bride and bridegroom face each other.

The bridegroom takes the bride's right hand in his, and says:
I, [Name], take you, [Name],
to be my wife,
to have and to hold
from this day forward,
for better, for worse,
for richer, for poorer,
in sickness and in health,
to love and to cherish,
till death us do part,
according to God's holy law,
and this is my solemn vow.

The bride takes the bridegroom's right hand in hers, and says:
I, [Name], take you, [Name],
to be my husband,
to have and to hold
from this day forward,
for better, for worse,
for richer, for poorer,
in sickness and in health,
to love and to cherish,
till death us do part,
according to God's holy law,
and this is my solemn vow.

Appendix 4

The giving of rings

The minister receives the ring(s), and says this prayer:
Heavenly Father, by your blessing let these ring be to [Name] and [Name] a symbol of unending love and faithfulness, to remind them of the vow and covenant which they have made this day through Jesus Christ our Lord.

All **Amen**.

The bridegroom places the ring on the fourth finger of the bride's left hand and holding it there, says:
[Name], I give you this ring
as a sign of our marriage.
With my body I honour you,
all that I am I give to you,
and all that I have I share with you,
within the love of God,
Father, Son and Holy Spirit.

If rings are exchanged, they loose hands and the bride places a ring on the fourth finger of the bridegroom's left hand and, holding it there says:
[Name], I give you this ring
as a sign of our marriage.
with my body I honour you,
all that I am I give to you,
and all that I have I share with you,
within the love of God,
Father, Son and Holy Spirit.

If only one ring is used, before they loose hands, the bride says:
[Name], I receive this ring
as a sign of our marriage.
With my body I honour you,
all that I am I give to you,
and all that I have I share with you,
within the love of God,
Father, Son and Holy Spirit.

Appendix 5

Suggested readings for your marriage service

Psalm 19, 84, 85, 91, 121, 139:1–18

Ecclesiastes 4:9–12

Song of Songs 8:6–7

Isaiah 40:25–31

John 2:1–11

John 15:1–4, 9–17

1 Corinthians 13:1–8(a)

Ephesians 3:14–21

Ephesians 5:21–33

Philippians 2:1–11

Colossians 3:12–17

1 John 4:7–16

Appendix 6

Recommended books

The Five Love Languages
by Gary Chapman (Moody Press, Northfield Publishing, 2015)

The Other Side of Love: Handling Anger in a Godly Way
by Gary Chapman (Moody Press, Northfield Publishing, 1999)

Boundaries in Marriage
by Dr Henry Cloud and Dr John Townsend (Zondervan, 2002)

Rules of Engagment: How to Plan a Successful Wedding/How to Build a Marriage that Lasts
by Richard and Katharine Hill (Lion Hudson Plc, 2009)

Look Before you Leap
by J. John (Authentic Lifestyle, 2004)

The Marriage Book
by Nicky and Sila Lee (Alpha International, 2009)

The Mystery of Marriage
by Mike Mason (Multnomah, 2005)

Loving Against the Odds
by Rob Parsons (Hodder & Stoughton, 2010)

The Sixty Minute Marriage
by Rob Parsons (Hodder & Stoughton, 2009)

A Celebration of Sex
by Douglas Rosenau (Thomas Nelson, 2002)

**The
Marriage
Preparation
Course**

If you are interested in finding out more about The Marriage Course
or The Marriage Preparation Course (designed for engaged couples),
where they are running or how to start up a course, please contact:

The Marriage Course Department
HTB Brompton Road
London SW7 1JA

Tel: **0845 644 7544**
Email: **info@themarriagecourse.org**
Website: **themarriagecourse.org**

If you are interested in finding out more about the Christian faith and
would like to be put in touch with your nearest Alpha, please contact:

The Alpha Office
HTB Brompton Road
London SW7 1JA

Tel: **0845 644 7544**
Website: **alpha.org**